THE BURIED
BREATH

About the Author

Ciarán O'Rourke was born in 1991 and took a degree in English and History at Trinity College, Dublin. He received a Masters in English and American Studies from Oxford in 2014, and is currently doing a doctorate on William Carlos Williams at his *alma mater* in Dublin. A winner of the *Lena Maguire / Cúirt New Irish Writing Award*, the *Westport Poetry Prize*, and the *Fish Poetry Prize*, his poems have appeared in a number of leading publications, including *Poetry Ireland Review*, *Poetry Review*, *The Irish Times*, *The London Magazine*, *New Welsh Review*, *The Spectator*, and *Irish Pages*. His pocket-pamphlet, *Some Poems*, was published as a Moth Edition in 2011.

THE BURIED BREATH

CIARÁN O'ROURKE

THE IRISH PAGES PRESS
2018

The Buried
Breath
is first published in hardback
on 1 November 2018.

The Irish Pages Press
129 Ormeau Road
Belfast BT7 1SH
Ireland

www.irishpages.org

Typeset in 14 / 18 pt Monotype Perpetua
Designed, composed and printed by Nicholson & Bass, Belfast

Dust-jacket photograph: Enri Canaj
Cover designs: Charles Gouldsbrough

A CIP catalogue record for this book
is available from The British Library.

ISBN: 978-0-9935532-2-6

To Mum and Dad
and to my sisters, Iseult and Aeveen.

CONTENTS

THE CURE FOR NETTLES

Near death, his arm would quiver
down the sheets,

the blood trails tracing black
along the vein,

and when I touched I held
a cooling heat

in both my hands,
and almost choked on air

to lift his nothing-weight
so easily,

his body thin, a brittle stick
that breathed,

the transformation near-complete
from when

he stepped with dock leaves
shooting from his grip,

to hoist me from the nettle patch,
and kneel,

and reconcile
my stinging limbs with green:

milk from the fist, a water-
coloured cure.

So here, I reach for him
and flounder still,

in loss that's more an element
than ill,

his voice
the silence that remains to say,

you felt the spirit blister
through the bark

that stiffened round me
as the minutes died,

but the final fever
cleared my eyes like rain.

HOSPICE

What poem
or prayer is there
to call this animal to heel,

that webs your body so,
and skulks
in every whrum of blood,

ready to feast
when you speak, or rise,
or raise an arm,

and what
bone-dull element
is need to us, who cannot alter

or undo
the rock-dumb motion
of this room,

which sways
to keep you
from the waking world:

the rigid chair, the rolling
desk, this week's flowers,
and the water glass.

Against the ugliness
your walls contrive,
these things grow still,

till all that's left
is the window
opposite your seat,

to which the bleak
rain beats,
and the wetting wind.

So think beyond,
to the sounds of home
and the carried sun,

to the high morning
begun again,
the water rustling

and the rain
still green —
to walk out

in summertime, a furl
of swallows lifting,
and the Barr Road bare.

We lean in, close
as breath to you,
and whisper news,

as if to make
grief ripple,
life break through,

to see you sit
without contagion,
your hands at ease,

or leave entirely,
your shadow flying
from the sickbed sheets,

like a sun-
set tremolo
seeping the sedge,

the corncrake
croaking love tomorrow
at the island's edge.

MAN KNEELING IN GRASS

Francis Bacon, 1952

It must be good
to fall like this
in some dark space
of the mind, and find
your body feeling, after all,
the total metaphor
of rushes and earth
grow to softness
across your knees
and rise, furring your arms
to the elbow
with the swish and smell
of meadow grass
and elemental ground.
Or perhaps
the swilling wish persists,
in this rectangular
corridor of night
I catch you in,
to sink through earth
and ache forever
in the well-deep nightmare
there, like stone.

Such grief, I think, could
only animate my own
small weight of need
in watching you: to send
the breeze of light
already trickling
through your scene
to flood the grass
and lift your mud-grey torso
from its shell. I might
hear you then, brother,
if you whispered
from your half-
factual meadow room,
that it is good
to have knelt
your body in the grass
like this, and grown
as actual in learning it
as darkness was,
as real and human
in the midnight hour
as any absence is.

BURYING TURNUS

Virgil, Aeneid XII, *ll.872-884; Juturna speaking*

Could I slow the sun, retain
the heat of seconds in the air,
let shadows tremble

round the dial, by art,
or skill, or barely human need,
to hold you here, my brother,

far from the gnash
of falling wings, from Death
the monster, and his calling lair,

to hold you back, brother,
from the gap you enter,
this darkness you've become – but how?

And how could a sister,
a nymph like me, a grieving girl,
a soul to flowing mosses

and to floods, how can I,
immortal as the rain, as swept
and washed with loss of you,

how will I beat the earth
to ease your limbs,
how heal the stillness

that you've sunk into,
the blood-shut eyes, the un-
responding mouth... what can I do?

And since you're gone
from fact and life, if not
from dreams – what god,

what murmur-loving listener,
in room or cloud, am I
forever speaking to?

Will your words repeal
the river? Your hands
scoop out

the spring-
suggesting ground?
If not to bring him back,

cleansing the hair,
the blinking skin, then
to lower me down,

down to the black, half-
empty, sleepless place,
where I might join

my brother, and
the disembodied others,
in the lonely heaven.

THE KILLING MARCH

In memory of Miklós Radnóti, 1909-1944

Each day permits
the old atrocities
anew –

the necessary deaths,
the far-off scream
come near,

the itch of madness
spreading
on the hands and hair.

History is one
disaster, feeding
off another, or:

what poems are made
to witness
and withstand.

You taught us that –
or someone did,
whose teaching stemmed

from what he saw,
from the hunger hushing
through him like a mist,

his head adrift
with grief, or sleep,
but not dead yet

on the killing march.
Against all murderous
decrees, and against

the unreturning cities
razed, the angel
drowning in the bricks,

the roads
where beggars roam
and drop, it's true:

the oak trees
still are breathing,
and the fist,

which ice and metal
hammered once,
can furl

to feel the winter
easing
in a luff of rain.

So it is, poet,
in this barbaric language,
built from pain,

I imagine echoings
to be enough
to raise

your sightless eyes
and famine face,
and faith

in breath, a force
to conjure
youth again –

that place
of which, you say,
the music speaks

in mutter-tongues
and morse. Love poet,
eternal pastoralist,

in the din of one more
ending world,
I commemorate your corpse.

POSTCARDS FROM PALESTINE

The tidy wars you planned
above my body's shrinking map,

the scars your bullet-mind unlatched,
and hatched, and loosed across my land,

the stench of metal on your boots,
the brutal compass in your hands,

(my south of buried villages,
my east of risen moons) –

they all go into it, shards
of the voice, or lines in the air,

into the remnant which you fear,
my torturer, will escape from here

to rectify the echoes, redirect the breeze…
that ghost, that almost emptiness,

in which your symphonies of dread
have dared me to believe.

~

We know our land
when the soldiers send us
to the border camps,

and press our mouths
into the ground.

We knew our home
when the fugue of drones
began to float,

rising, falling,
above the roof.

We'll know our names
from the numbers
they assign to us,

our every death apportioned
by a decimal of grief.

~

Not the body only,
but my poetry
and dreams they killed —

the presidents and generals,
the governments
of nations,

the scientists
and educators
standing to attention,

the nimble-
minded bureaucrats
whose fingers typed extinction.

I mark them all
as profiteers
of massacre and rubble.

And to the others,
opening clear windows
to tomorrow's sun, I say:

look for me
among the vanished faces
of my people.

~

Remember my words,
as if they were warmed by the blood in my wrist,
as if they were cut from the coil of my tongue.

Remember my song,
as if it contained the bricks of my city,
or rang with the sound of the sea on the rocks,
as if it resisted a world without pity,
or was wrung from the breath of my life's skeleton.

Remember the sun
that lent me a shadow to plant in the ground,
that gave me the right to delight in the clouds,
that watched as I fell at the flash of the bombs,
that burns on the flesh of the bone-brittle homes.

Remember my poems,
as if in accusation of the architects of pain
when seeking for the future that the olive branch proclaims.

CRUCIFIXION
Matthias Grünewald, 1516

So god
is in the knucklebone,

in the nipple, the rib,
the shoulders splayed,

in the shrapnel nailed
to nerves and flesh,

in the speckle and gash
of blood on the wind;

and god is hot
with plague and rot,

in the hunger
hulling out the hands,

in the clamour clotting
through the throat,

in the metal moon
while the drowning boat

of anger, body,
hope gives out;

and god is loud
in the starless muck,

is blue as sorrow,
is a bruise of rock,

is true, is close,
as burning sleet,

is the emblem killed
by the magistrate;

and god is what
persists and dies

in the murdered voice,
the broken eyes:

is fever, night-
mare, unrelief,

is the silent death,
the hollow grief;

and god is lit
by fact and myth

that vision draws
from twisted sheets,

from the dirt, from the dark,
from bone and limb,

from the earthen lips
that meet and stiffen,

and the weeping feet
as huge as heaven.

FRESH AIR

Winslow Homer, 1878

The wind grows new forever
on this hilltop, as I watch
the leaves swim backwards
in their cave-deep daub
of cloud behind you, loving
how the soar of sun you stand in
perfects the bright dial
of your shoe buckles, and spills
into the lapse your hands inhabit
quietly as shells. The greatest
loveliness might be now,
though, when I see slowly
how this sudden freshness
has heaved through everything
the portrait pictures,
except your gaze — you are
here and elsewhere
in the same escaping breath.
Or imagining, after,
that perhaps you wake to it
when the picture finishes,
this ordinary thought you hold,

which the painter wondered
into sunlit nearness, so
you are real and remote
in the way that gull shape is,
lingering high above
your dreaming head,
flung to the world
in a veer of blue.

MARTELLO

Sun out
on the sea path
and a grey wave rising
in my chest
as I wade with you
into an April tide,
watching two terns
dangle the breeze
before their one
pure, spearing dive
through water,
which I miss in my
less elegant attempt,
rushing the element
in a sudden gulp
of need, and thinking,
as my body learns
itself again
in the tidal seep
of ice through limbs,
that you and I
were made for this
old beat of want

the sea imprints each year
on sandy minds,
that a bare-backed,
part-painful ritual like this
can be as clear
as water, and is best,
knowing the heavy
ocean-pull of life
to be both now
and here, in the fish-quick
dart and dip
of our own two hearts,
human still,
and swimming
into Spring.

FOR A GARDEN SLUG

The
  long
    vowel
    the grass
    makes
    of your body
     takes the shape
  of music in our eyes
  as you pull away
   from sudden
    sun-pools your
    fluent love of
    stone and grass,
     your liquid purr
      and fingering of
      the green blades
     becoming the words
      a cello might
      have known
      before the touch
     of human hands
     as you move, one
    perfecting limb,

to form verbs
of petal hush
and the dull mud,
as if to render
visible in this space
a whisper of
the quiet,
quavered
shadow light
you speak,
mouthing
in the slow
passage
of your trail
the soft truths
which slugs
can sing:
here is

m   m

y   y
b   s
o   o
d   n
y   g

THE REVOLUTIONIST

Variations on poems by Roque Dalton, 1935-75

And so I say the earth
is beautiful,

and belongs
like poetry or bread

to all of us,
who despite love's

poisoned battleground
are believers still

in the pungent roots
that smell like tears,

in the streaming grain
of tomorrow's skies,

in the billowing verb
of the blood we share –

we who have faced
the hungry future singing,

the earth belongs to all of us,
like poetry, like bread.

~

My sweat has the soil and the dew,
and the labour and dust,
and the stink of everything I own in it.

It has the vapid grey heat
of midnight grief, thick on the tongue.
It has the taste of a village dead by drought

in a month of promised rains.
It has the mist a man turns into slowly
when his body rots in the muck.

It has the sweet breeze of my country,
riffling the log-books
of silence and catastrophe.

So I'm like some weightless animal
that stalks abandoned streets and towns,
the sound of massing voices

ringing round me as I roam:
I'll die of this sweat the world invents
to keep those voices down.

~

Something's changed:
the dead are speaking up.

They ask us questions
that we can't forget,

as if we filled their mouths
with marble once,

but now the marble's
singing wind;

or as if the beat
of dancing rifle butts

was never all there was –
and now the dead

are clamouring,
no longer happy to remain

the silent
and growing majority.

~

Who built the fleet of blazing cities,
who left, who stayed, who brought

the perfect walls of parliaments to life
by hand and sinew-song,

who bartered their bodies continually
in *Happyland* and *Cave of Dreams*,

who begged for more, who ran away,
who crossed the fence en masse, subtle as a fox,

whose faces scorched the wind, who burned,
who crumpled in the dirt when bullets rang,

who grew grey-lipped and bevel-brained
in cells for thieves and murderers,

in butcher-chambers glistening every night
through all the marching nations of the land,

who walked the seething hills for work,
who conquered daylight's spinning map

by dreaming every breath, who staggered
pissed or half-malarial down death's unbroken alley,

the fuckwits, dropouts, retchers
of the bitter earth, whose mouths

were beautiful, but always empty,
whose laughter split the skies, and will,

the saddest people in the world – I mean you,
my friends, my fellow citizens, children of the sun.

~

Call me a communist
        and you'll know my nature:

the urge and ache (perennial)
        of permanent revolution

that permeates my mind. It's great!
        And never dies, this pain

a-flutter in the gut and brain,
        history's living scar.

If you ask me: capitalism sits
        like a belching toad

on the drowning leaf
        we call the world.

If you ask me: the world
        we have's an engine,

dumping bodies in the dark.
        If you ask me: paradise

on earth's no dream, but lurks
        in every pulse of breath

our arms and lips
        were born to learn.

Call it communism — a natural
        pain-killer, the size of the sky.

GUATEMALA, 1967

In memory of Otto René Castillo, 1936-1967

Say nation,
and the deer and moon
unlatch a shadow;

the darkness
quickens;
a candle blows.

Say water,
and thirst assumes
a human shape:

the man
whose mouth
defied the desert,

whose lips
the owners of the rain
would govern,

whose throat
the street-patrolling
prison guards would smash.

Say pain,
and the concrete
barracks' walls

are politic with light:
in the blood-loud night
the shutters glisten,

the darkened windows
flash and gleam;
next door, nearby,

across the world, a thousand
silences conspire
to regulate the scream.

Say beauty,
and perhaps, my love,
I'll find your form again,

my tongue journeying
the valleys, my fingers
rivering the slopes

in search of quietness,
of storms,
and the real dawn

always gaining,
to burn the blue half-
sleep of it to air…

or perhaps it's you
I'll see, my country,
with a hope grown vivid

at the edge of vision:
in the slum, in the mud,
on the stricken hills,

in the book of laughter,
in the nameless streets,
in the fists

of language lifting
with the stars and sun,
in the flickered flame.

Say poetry,
and the voices
of the sick

might rise tomorrow,
the faces of the earth
might smile.

LOVE SONG

The sun of sleep is rising in your head,
the colour of plum love, and spoon-bright,
as the two moons that held me
close to crescents with a sigh, and sink.

The whisper softens to a breath.
In the pane above you, veils of web
window in mid-hum
the pendulum of a robin's hovering.

And if you were to waken now
under the far skies of this thought,
then you would know I made it for you,

that in the plum-dark wings of a robin
I heard a summer singing
and dreamed again of your limbs.

SEA STONES

Why try trace
a footprint in the breeze

this way, an echo
furled in dust and air?

The broken shore
was ours alone,

leaning in
to one another

as the water whispered
and the starlight fell.

~

Fresh from the sea,
cicadas singing
in our heads,

we surveyed the kingdom
we had climbed away from,

the vineyards lush
with martyrs' blood,

Charlemagne's dream
of earth-lit oceans

rising round us
in the summer heat.

~

Higher still,
a flock of sea birds

dragged its net
across the sun, omen

of a sky all swelt
with foreign rains,

which soon
moved in,

the dark air
trembling

with an eye-
blue light.

~

My sight strung
to the kite
of your back,

long and lovely
and supple with
spindrift, the seas

breaking across my
feet, and you
in the turn

and sway of
it all, spooling
me close, through

the burning wind.

~

Days after you go,
a storm invades
the midnight air:

shruggle of thunder
on the shoreline, sea stones
rattling the pane.

Pausing to write you
a note of it, I find

a small bird
still hurtles
in its cage,

bullows its wings
against my heart.

~

The sun's empire
will be safe forever
on this frontier

of red roof tiles
and olive walls,
these rooms

to which
we may return
sometime,

to grow old
at last
in the long nights.

SUNLIGHT

William Orpen, 1925

Try as I might
to follow
the slow geometries
of flesh – from
your dipping leg,
along your hip,
to the pink
perfection of your neck –
catching every detail,
possessing the always
fuller picture
of your loops and lines,
you continue
to elude the graph,
your face
a delicate elision,
your fingers dim
in their pertinent work,
your breasts
half-hidden
by light's transparent
easing into place,
sliding like an ill-

timed lover
through the window
and impolitely
turning up the colours
as it goes,
so each drape
and naked rumple
of the furniture
has come to match
the pallor
of the sun on skin,
and the flounce
of sweat-black hair
above your ear
grows clear,
as if suggesting
what shade and stocking
on your outstretched foot
conceal –
your shadow spaces,
lush still, and secreted,
for all the morning's
baring heat…
reminder, perhaps,
of the eye
that yearns for

what the skin remembers,
or that flame-
dark blaze, which
returns as water
to the window pane
next day,
to fill each crack
and crinkle
that the night laid plain,
washing the room
with want again.

ON WITTGENSTEIN'S STEP

The Botanic Gardens, Dublin

You have stayed with me all morning,
and now we rest in the glasshouse:

you, seated on stone beside
the pineapple plants, looking
elsewhere

while I wait, dull in the drowse
the light makes spin across
the leaf life of this place,

reading that Wittgenstein once
loved to find the step where
you are now, and sit.

I can picture him, stranger
at the rim of things, letting
the ebb of fruit play out
its shape within these walls,

solitary as we two
find ourselves to be,
and yet at ease, perhaps,
to have wandered wondering
to this spot.

Perhaps, too, he found
something like the tremolo
we've made in air together here,
some symmetry of mind
in the supple arc of stems,

or found himself
captivated by some space
pale and soundless
as what you mould in me,
the nape of your neck
unfurling through me
like a breath
I cannot utter
or contain,
but only feel
as what is given
and is good.

To the glass about us
the trees give up their
temperatures of sound,

but send, also, your silence
through my own,
scattering my thoughts
like rain.

All morning we have been growing
to the loss we fall to now,
                    into a lightness
for which we have no language
but ourselves,

dreaming by the step, heads
tipped and knees tilted
to a touch we neither of us
notice, both being diffident
in all but knowing
we are near.

That though we will pick up
our paths again, our voices shining
where we walk, for this instant
we must live only by the grammars
of our need, and love....

So I turn to you, ghost of a thinker,
with your thoughts that move beyond
the windowed stillness of that wish,
and say,

when we forget again
this hushed oblivion,
which for a moment
we have shared,

speak to us of
what you saw;

in this remembering, come close
and whisper it,

let the sky-limbed world grow green
against the domes once more,
and sing perfectly
in its way

of what it was
we had become.

POSTSCRIPT

Catullus, LXVIII B

But I cannot keep in quietness
the name of this one friend
of mine, Allius,

or let all time ahead
forget his kindness to me,
and to many,

or lay that kindness
in the darker plot
of unremembered hours,

so I say it plainly,
here, to you, as to a god
who lives by whispered air,

to carry the page
this name grows old within
to a thousand others

listening in tomorrow's
brightened room,
where Allius

may still be known,
and the spider spinning there
its veil of breath

withhold her web
from the memory
of my friend.

For, more than once,
he gave me ease
and helped my mind

when I was fitful,
burning in the gorge,
my body rock-dull

in a scorch of tears,
eyes all sick with salt
and face raw red,

in a rain of want,
my lover gone.
Allius

was like a breeze
that lifts the muttered prayer
of sailors

into sky, scattering
the sea-deep storm
with light,

or like the water-
falling glint
of water in the sun,

its moss-lit clearness
flowing to wet
the fingertips

of two heat-
bitten travellers,
stooping on the track.

Allius, my friend,
was this to me,
when he unlatched

the field gate
on a barely beaten lane
to the house he left

unlocked for us,
that room to which
all yearning strayed:

my lover's footstep,
treading the doorway
and pale in shade,

her sandal softly
creaking
on the sill...

as soft, perhaps, as one
who walked in the same
slow heat of need

another time:
Laodamia,
whose husband's half-

built house of love
remained a soldier's
early work, and last,

and who once, at daybreak,
untwined both arms
from his boyish neck,

to rise from the bed
that they had drifted
all the winter in,

and feel
a colder flame
at work on air,

the fainter
urge of war
for flesh,

and the bone-deep
vanishing it was to bring
to husbands

in the Trojan dust,
like a tremble
out of light, that day,

a sense too slight
to wake him yet,
but near enough

to alter
easiness in her,
as she pauses

by the bridal bed
at morning, far from the un-dug
graves of Troy...

Troy, Allius,
where my brother
was also lost of light,

taking
into alien ground
his high parade of dailiness,

the brittle joys
Laodamia must
have known

and missed in hers,
a lack in the abundance,
usual as rain —

as her passion proved,
pulling her down
to a seep of emptiness

when he was gone,
bottomless as the earth
to which all waters reach,

and yet an ordinary pain,
and one that, in my way,
I understand.

To see always my love,
like some goddess
come close, pale

in the saffron
drape of dark,
and yet to know her

not for me alone,
me as one of many,
the hunger-haunted poet,

Catullus
of stray midnights,
and not the marriage bed!

Though the give-and-take
can be enough
to live in touch, and learn,

each day a sky-
white stone to keep,
weighted in the palm.

Yes, Allius, you say
you knew all this before,
but know, too,

that should tomorrow
and forever
take from you your name,

or leave your lifeline
rusting in the rains
of time,

in return
for the gifts of love
you gave, my friend,

this song of mine
is given
with the wish,

new now,
and now eternal,
that your love and you go softly,

in a light
akin to what
your kindnesses allowed,

to that unshadowed way
I lived my life
a while with her,

whose living
even now makes sweet
the endless

bitterness of night.

COYOTE
Sean Scully, 2000

When you've turned
to the glur of dust on the pane,
and held a prairie
howling in your brain,

when you've watched
the winter prowling on the grass,
and stood, and wondered,
at the shaking glass,

or seen the rain
unravel gravel beds,
the graves re-wrapped
and wrung in sheeting wind,

or chased the shape
of shadow light at night,
your breath
a living creature in the room,

when you've heard the moon
resolve the ticking shore,
a wooden song
subside beneath the boards,

you'll know, by then,
the hunger in my heart,
that moves the dark
disorder into form

and still impels
this rhythm in my arm.
So hold to it,
and follow where it bids,

let hands pursue
the pulse, the fading trails,
and when
the final ordinance prevails

you plant the vista
in the humming grid.

TO THE LAST OLD POET
ON EARTH

When you cannot sing at midnight
as the moon-deep window
darkens, and the trees blow
on the far avenues
of San Francisco, speak your words
instead, as slowly as you can,
growing beautifully older
with each low syllable,
until the air is a page
as ancient as you are,
quivering and bare
with the need you filled tonight
for a voice with breath in it,
and this way, the dead light
of galaxies still will fall
on the alleyways
where our listening bodies
hold back gently
to wonder at that firm frailty
in the wind they felt, and much
later, as we wake by dawn
to see the pale flame

flicker on the world
and the sun-soft window
glow with air more nearly
than we knew, but not
unknown, we might
say gladly to ourselves
that we dreamt this once,
and think of you, old poet,
on your last earth,
speaking to the stars.

OXFORD

No sea like Dublin's ocean
here. Only seagulls soaring
in the eye-deep air,

and my body netted
in an onward kind
of falling motion.

~

Sky seemed meadow-lit
in Rose Lane.

I felt bound for bridges
each time I passed, eyes
swept and rinsed
in the language of weathervanes,
all of me striding to some
new life
inside my own.

But I was standing still,
the city a sinkening
through time around me,
a vanished map
my mind moved through
like light in a glass,
or breath in rain.

Once, a blackbird cried out
from a dark century, unseen,

and I knew it then — that poems
take root where ghosts have been.

~

Catholics in corridors
of earth beneath our feet.

Two hours before dawn,
as chaotic gaiety
dimmed from one window
to another,
we could hear them,
pillaging the stillness
under Cromwell's boots,
the cobbles wet
with war and rain.

As the dawn sniffed close
to Mary's hem,
their laughter muffled on
like gunpowder.

Even now they were waiting,
growing more raucous
by the hour

in their gleeful,
unholy dark.

~

Leaving Portmeadow
for home again
was to part my image
of ancient earth
from things that grew in it.

I wanted to forget
the inhuman grasses
mounding in my memory;

to shake off
the dung-blue geese
with their grey flowerings
of flight at night.
But my mind moved closer
to the very ripple
I had tried to sever:

the whole dead meadow,
alive in a bloom
of stagnant water.

~

How many books
to write the world?

Everyone back to their rooms,
each to the huddle
of his room-like head.

For we are learning ourselves again,
running right into the mind
in a daily gust,

and dropping all the maps...

CATULLUS

Catullus, dawn-young and delicate as rain,
I thank a thousand gods I never met you.
For days you've lingered, brazen on the corners,
hot-fingering your puny cock, screaming love
to some piss-pale heaven, under which love poems
burst impossibly from life-embezzled beds.
I listen with avoiding eyes, knowing you
well. Though soon, your naked languages of light
and dark, hate-ridden rapture, will quieten
to pure signatures on the wind you face
with your open tunic now, and your bared heart.
It's then, old friend, strange as the moon at dusk,
we others will search decrepit alleyways
for your corpse, and come home scavengers of rain,
alive in the dreams you moved among, mourning.

STILL LIFE OF PEACHES AND FIGS

Paul Cézanne, 1890

This time
I'm sending peaches,
and a summer's sun
that dawdles in
on last year's kitchen
where the plates
are never empty.

Pure vowels
of the unperfected
morning, they are
lain or left out
in whatever
slow tumble
of fruitfall
they fell from,
casual as rain.

And figs! Echo-
shaped, but so sure
in their small
altering of light,
they remake
the room entirely.

Oh love, I know:
all of this you've heard
already, and words
are not round or heavy
in the way fruit is,
nor soft enough
to satisfy the mouth
or fill the aching palm.

Only, it was not the fruit
of poems that I was sending,
but another easy, breathing,
blemishable thing.

The thought, perhaps,
which if I wished enough
would sail through years
of oceanic air
unchanged,

or need of mine,
which might rain through
a sea-bright room
as stirred to life
as this one is,
to fall, by some half-
miracle of love
or hunger,
whole at last
into your open hands.

WHEN YOU GET HERE

Let the geese fly north,
and the mind of this river
ring with their high
honking through air,
and as its mud-long
nuzzling limb
goes quietening
the banks after,
let the river slowly
piece this place
to a low and lull again,
and the meadow
grow back
into itself
as the wings wane.
Let water restore
one peace, then another,
in gradual ways,
till sameness settles
and all is tilting
into stillness
as before –
only, when
you get here,

save a space
for one thing new:
I mean, that echo
at the edges,
trembling still,
when my heart
heard wings
on the river path,
and I called
for days
to you.

FROM THE NOTEBOOK OF ONCE MODERN TIMES

Variations on poems by Rubén Darío, 1867-1916

Stay long enough in one place, –
dark-haired at morning, on a binge-blue road,

or still and slow as roses growing
in the rose-lit garden (your heart as slow),

in the gust of a doorframe, giving way
to dust and wind and the weight you put to it,

in the sweat of lust, in the rain of love,
at the beating rim of an eagle's song, –

and the silhouettes you'd thought
were ghosts assemble, the metaphors

invade your flesh and vision,
translate the air to shallow breath.

Stay long enough in one place
and shadows lengthen, rumours sift,

and the hawk you watched for all your life
is neither bird nor prey, but here it sings:

life's last hornet, dark as death,
honing close to kiss or sting.

~

The only way

is to know by motion,
to feel, to fuck,

to have no faith,
or nothing but.

To expand your lungs,
extend the list

of lips desired,
dreams possessed

(bow down to Whitman,
resist the rest).

To believe the brain
outlives the skull,

the shell retains
the ocean's soul.

To embark, imbibe,
envision verse,

collect it all
in laughter first.

To praise the symbol
with the fact —

the swan in a drift
of evening air,

guest of the world
and flying west.

To understand:
that the man alone

and stranded,
howling to the sun,

has always
been your future,

and you must move on.

THE HELMET MAKER

Attic detail, 480 BC

One ankle betrays
the unserenity in this
tranquil summer heat
you sit through, each
assuring angle of your
helmet maker's poise
at peace with the work
your hands adhere to,
except for that one
mass of bone, that
bulge at the neck
of your planted foot.
Whatever pulse the pain
injects through air
must be frailer
than the pale rain
of swallows lifting
in some far field
of the mind, to
whomever it is who
glimpsed you here –
you could almost
convince us

of the ease of making
metal graceful
for the war
erupted always
in another Corinth
outside your room,
though close, perhaps,
to this scooped
window of the world
we watch you through.
As it is, you stare right
past the dead eye-
slits of the helmet
your arm grows into
like a branch, and
your ankle swells,
as if rooting you
forever to the pause
this hurt has made
its dwelling in –
before the scalpel
that you brandish dips,
and the visage yields
to the last incision.

DEATH OF A REFUGEE

List me down when I am dead,
and may the list include
the bird that fled,

the bomb that flew,
the avenues buckled
and blit with dust —

mourn if you must,
but let no elegist
intrude, to bury

the words you knew
for murder, the laws
you wrote to kill,

the years you watched
me trammelled,
and the broken book

my body filled.
Have history inhere
in the border singing

through my head,
in the blood
that bled

at the tick of your pen,
in the bullet, the brick,
the burning air,

in the char you made
of children,
the cartographers you trained

to map my eyes
with shrapnel, to wrap
my feet in flame.

Poetry is feverish,
memory an art,
so say

that I kept living,
though you ripped
my world apart,

and remember me
as human, in your
hardly human heart.

RECOLLECTIONS OF AN EMIGRÉ

Variations on poems by Antonio Machado, 1875-1939

Tonight I'm thinking of the war again,
its shatter and spin of eyes and limbs
on the rooftops, bridges, sun-bare hills;

and thinking of the song it shreds
in wheat fields, cities, and the breath it steals
from quiet streets, to scatter as death

on the burning farms – death, which I see
has time, tonight, to pause here, too,

to pluck a lemon from the hanging bough,
which quivered in the wind, as the sun withdrew.

~

From the earth, from visions,
from the gravel roads,

from dust in the breeze,
from bones, from blood,

from the risen flame
as the morning sings,

from the half-heard voice
on the flooding verge,

from the pummelled gut
when the rifles bark,

from the clear-eyed heat
of the corpse's gaze,

raise hymns, raise anthems
to the man the bullets buried…

Lorca, as the bombs chant on
to hunt your elegy,

Grenada's chorus
will lift its fists

and call the city yours.

~

Did you see the sky today?
Or, as I did, the bell jar

of sky-refracting light and rain,
globed above the compact fields?

Something woke and sent me to it,
flinging the windows, un-
battening the heart!

There among the cypresses,
in the lemoned haze of garden and summer,
you stood, as if returned

from a rain-lit morning, the whole air
wet around us, and your face a-gleam.

I felt it all come back today,
as if no longer vanished, nor a dream.

~

In my country, to live
is to want to live

between a Spain that rots
and a Spain that yawns.

You, who are new
to the world, and fresh:
look to your god, or run quick,

for one Spain or the other
will cause your heart
to icen up, and break.

~

It's time to fashion songs
the world might share,

as if to sing were knowing
knowledge impotent
on the seas we all go under, in the end.

Or as if the key we needed
was the one we lack, and every lock a whimper
in the blood and brain.

So sing, you songsters! Though no beam
of light can thud the earth
but the lines evaporate, or fade…

What is it words say, after all?
And what the water, from the fluent rock?

~

These days death
goes on, and life abides.

And our part, too,
is partly death:

to die, but
to die building

our paths across the sea.

~

That swarm bedamned –
of poets cricketing love-tunes
to an empty moon!

I'll keep company instead
with this one who walks
beside me in the dark.

For he says that those
who speak in solitude, like him,
hope also, in their way,
to talk to god.

~

Would you lead me again
down the white track,
my hand in yours, our voices
free in the noon-deep air?

As I cross and re-cross
the shattered plazas now,
the shadows vivid,
the cart wheels splintered
by their load,

I turn from the broken vista
to that place in sight
of mountains,

where your heartbeats still
are whispering, like wings.

~

When we were sleeping, maybe,
that hand hummed high once more,

which once sowed darkness
with the seeds of stars,

and this time
sent a music through it:

a strum-note echo
on the sea's guitar,

which reached and rippled
through us, as a sound

or two, a single word,
that trembled on our lips

and spoke the truth.

~

I loved you once, old shack.

She lived in you
        like spring
in the air a plane tree makes.

Now the stone's
wind-wickered
        at your side,
and to look
into your heart

is like blowing breath
into a cage:

the dust rubbles
round itself
in the breeze.

But up, see:
cold moons
        touch
in the windowpane...

and there am I,
going out again,
naked and unhappy,
        to roam
the ancient street.

COMBING THE HAIR (LA COIFFURE)

Edgar Degas, 1896; for my sisters

Days burn out; our inner life persists –
so this wall as red as a bursting fruit
could be a metaphor
for pain and sweetness both combined,
the easy, spreading wave of touch

a hairbrush tugs through all the room,
where soon you'll shindy from your seat
as the ritual completes, your hair
a flaring melody released
by the comber's tactful hands, her face

like yours a paragon
of second thoughts and soft abidance,
her deft, attending stance
the light
that sets your laughing arms aglow –

which leaves the watcher only
to depict, who keeps concealed
his stillness in the dance,
though every window's
singing now

his dream of praise, his passing glance.

THE PRISONER
Photograph of Keith Douglas, 1920-1944

The photographer
has shot too soon,
so you'll stand

like this forever:
unappeased
and reticent,

your uniform heat-
creased, eyes widened
for the rain

that may fall daily there
to burn a thrumming life
to dust.

Finding you this way,
opened onto
on a page your diffidence defies,

the past becomes
what later
knowledge lacks,

the fact
before the story
of the fact, perhaps,

or the watch-strap
tightened
on a boyish wrist,

and the man
not checking it
as the camera strikes.

And yet, to look again,
there is space, too, behind
your fierce unreadiness

for softness
to unfold itself, enough
even for the poet

to stir in this image
of soldier, son, and lover still,
and show

which verve of air
and coolness out of earth
were yours that day,

and which our own
in the blank
we think to recollect.

Wanting you
so remembered, I feel
that I could wait

a thousand hours
for your gun-dark gaze
to clamber

out of the stifled light
you're wrapped inside,
and blink un-

photographed,
near with words,
on the heat-forgiven sand.

A fly enters the room
in which these wishes writhe,
lights on the hand

that would grip time's net
like this, and shake you
out of it, lithe with life.

For an instant, history
is an insect, caressing skin,
and what poetry there was

vanishes, in which you'd lift
your frantic cigarette
to mouth, and speak.

Learning from your reticence,
I know
that when this creature

escapes the brittle cage
of my attention
I may return

to press the living weight
of breath
impossibly through air

until your
almost poetic
poet self walks free.

Though, as I look
from your unmoving
portrait now,

it seems that being true
to that half-gentle, grim-
lipped glance you give,

I must note with care
this fly that squats
so curiously

on the slope
of my wrist –
yes, and try

to replicate
the immense, inhuman
watchfulness

in its tiny poise,
its eyes and fingers
beautifully unfearful

of what my bone-
dull hand conveys:
a stillness

total as your picture's is,
but riddled also
with heat

in the mind, the sun-
caught suddenness there,
and the blood-beats.

ELEGY

Catullus, CI

To fling your death
on the hundred winds,

to recite your dust
in the lapsing wave,

to loose your bones,
to lieve your lips,

to stand in a sun-dim
mist of prayer,

to be
without you, brother,

a shadow gnawing
on the vanished air,

my voice the rain
that journeys here

continually, to sing
the dirt, to lift the seas,

to bring the ancient
gifts to ground,

like the urn upheld,
and the aching throat,

the buried breath
on the risen road,

the stone in the heart,
or the golden cup

which now
I proffer, brother,

raise to greet
your dark embrace –

to meet your sightless
silence with my own.

ACKNOWLEDGEMENTS

This collection took on its present shape thanks in large part to the editorial care and encouragement of Chris Agee. I am grateful to him, as well as to Jennifer, Jacob, and all the crew at The Irish Pages Press for their expertise and guidance.

Some of the poems included here previously appeared in the following: *Cyphers*, *Earthlines*, *Icarus*, *Irish Pages*, *New Welsh Review*, *Poetry Ireland Review*, *The Bogman's Cannon*, *The Galway Review*, *The London Magazine*, *The Stinging Fly*, and *The Stony Thursday Book*. Thanks are due to the editors of those publications, and also to the curators of the following poetry competitions and festivals, in which some of these poems won or were shortlisted for prizes: *The Westport Poetry Prize 2015 (In Memory of Dermot Healy)*, *The Bailieborough Poetry Festival 2015* and *The Fish Poetry Prize 2016*. I express my gratitude to the An Chomhairle Ealaíon / The Irish Arts Council for the literature bursary awarded to me in 2013.

I am indebted to Ken Keating for his editorial direction while working on the online chapbook, *The Sea Path* (Smithereens Press, 2016). Likewise, I reserve a special note of acknowledgement for Rebecca O'Connor, who gave me my first reading and then published a pocket-pamphlet of my poems in her *Moth Edition* series in 2011. I wish to thank (somewhat belatedly): Heather Brett, whose annual *Windows* anthology has been a source of encouragement to many a young writer; Hugo Williams, who responded with kindness and cogency to some of my early work and offered important advice to an emerging poet who felt he needed none; and Robert MacFarlane, similarly.

To my grandparents and family, I send my love. I am also glad to be able to mention here: my friends, especially Charlie and Nick, and my many teachers over the years for their various encouragements. To Charlie I owe my extended acquaintance with Catullus *LXVIII* and the work of Miklós Radnóti, the fruit of which may at least partly be found in this collection.

Throughout the writing of these poems, I have enjoyed the love, support, and good company of my immediate family. This book is dedicated to them.